My Dear Wildflower

r.h. Sin

Andrews McMeel
PUBLISHING®

Also by r.h. Sin

Whiskey Words & a Shovel

Whiskey Words & a Shovel II

Whiskey Words & a Shovel III

Rest in the Mourning

A Beautiful Composition of Broken

Algedonic

Planting Gardens in Graves

Planting Gardens in Graves Volume Two

Planting Gardens in Graves Volume Three

She Felt Like Feeling Nothing

Empty Bottles Full of Stories

She Just Wants to Forget

Falling Toward the Moon

We Hope This Reaches You in Time

A Crowded Loneliness

She's Strong, but She's Tired

She Fits Inside These Words

Winter Roses after Fall

Dream, My Child

Anywho, I Love You

I Hope She Finds This

I Hope This Reaches Her in Time Revised Edition

Come Back to Me

This Day Is Dark

Beautiful Sad Eyes, Weary Waiting for Love

Ascending Assertion

A Midnight Moon

The Year of Letting Go: 365 Days Pursuing Emotional Freedom

Andrews McMeel Publishing
a division of Andrews McMeel Universal
1130 Walnut Street, Kansas City, Missouri 64106

www.andrewsmcmeel.com

25 26 27 28 29 TEN 10 9 8 7 6 5 4 3 2 1

ISBN: 978-1-5248-9323-1

Library of Congress Control Number: 2024949968

Extended, scene one

you're waiting aren't you
you're always waiting for a sign
something that'll help you believe
in him and all of his lies

you're in denial about the truth
never questioning his excuse
say you think highly of yourself
but you still entertain his abuse

what happened to your soul
i see the bruises and the scars
he never deserved to touch your canvas
how'd you forget that you are art

i know it fucking hurts
but i'll just say this because it's true
any man who hurts your heart
is incapable of falling for you

and i know somewhere you agree
this is the hardest lesson learned

thought it was cool to play with fire
but no one warned you that it'd burn

now all the promises are broken
you cut yourself on shards of lies
smiling in every selfie
but inside you scream and cry

now what's a heart to do
when it aches black and blue
you put trust in his hands
but now his hands are harming you

there is love, i hope you find it
it lives within, i hope you find it
that text says, "baby i miss you"
but i hope you know he's lying

think of me a friend
or a stranger who gives a fuck
i just wish to see you grow
i'm tired of seeing you stuck

this moment is critical
there are things you need to do
your heart is in the wrong place
think of somewhere else to move

you've been patient
for a minute
you love them
yeah, i get it

but the pain
remains persistent
you hurt yourself
trying to fix it

there's misery in a love
that doesn't live up
to what you've dreamed
invisible to your beloved
you feel alone
and rarely seen

you cling to what's familiar
but you deserve so much more
waiting for them to change
but you're the one
worth waiting for

it's important
that you know this
so i wrote it
so you can see it

but none of this will matter
if you read it
and don't believe it

———————————————

i'm not perfect
i have flaws
i've made mistakes
but you don't get to keep me
from being loved
because you'd rather
hold a grudge
and i don't have to wait around
for you as if you're the only chance
at love i'll ever get

_____

i think about the gardens that bloom despite who is watching
or the sun that decides to rise
even when eyes are closed
and the people are asleep
i think about the moon
and the way it finds light
unafraid of the dark
alone in the night sky
but comfortable in the solitude
i think about the way
the birds sing
with no need for an audience
or how life itself goes on
not waiting for permission
i think about the galaxy
and the way it stretches on
reaching further into itself
or how existence keeps existing
or how symphonies
continue playing
even if no one is listening
i think of all of this
when i think about you

---

too often
they love the body
while neglecting the heart
that gives it life

too often
they focus on the skin
while ignoring the soul

they won't see you
for who you truly are
misusing you out of ignorance
as you are and will always be
beyond their comprehension

———————————

a relationship is like a lotus
under the wrong light
it begins to wilt
without proper care

_____

a relationship
will never bloom
sitting beneath
the light of a lie

---

it's just that when
the other person
is out of tune
in love's orchestra
the entire harmony suffers
and so you must
pick up your instrument
and leave

_____

a woman's heart is a well of life
and sometimes, it has to break
to nurture the seeds
of something new and beautiful

———————————————

she wept rivers
so that harmful things
could flow out of her life

———————————

she could never
fear the fire
she was
forged
by one

---

significant whispers
leaving an imprint
on her very essence

words followed by actions
that calm her soul
she wanted, she wants
she deserves
to be awakened
by a voice she can trust

wishing it to be me
i preserved my words
for the only one who will
appreciate them
waiting for the opportunity
to give her life and love
with my tongue

———————————

How did you get here? How in the hell did this happen? Your heart is sinking; you've been overthinking. Your heart is heavy, and you've been tired. How did you get here? Maybe you fell for him because of the manipulation. Maybe you fell for him because you were lonely. Maybe you fell for a man who couldn't love you because of his ability to tell you everything you wanted to hear at the exact time that you needed to hear it. Here you are reading this, looking for a sign or maybe a reminder of what you should look for instead. You can't hate yourself for being able to love someone without conditions—your ability to love someone unconditionally is truly a blessing, and maybe this failure in finding a love that lasts is a lesson, regardless of where you are or how bad it feels. I need you to understand that you are worthy of more, you deserve so much more, and you are strong enough to hold out until you get what you truly deserve: a love that won't force you into sadness. A love that won't cause you to compromise your own well-being for someone who will never care for you in the way you've longed for. I need you to begin looking into yourself for everything you need and more. I need you to remember your power and your ability to overcome all things and anything that comes against you. I need you to understand this doesn't have to be your life; I need you to want more for yourself. I need you to understand that this happens often and that you are not alone here. In fact, there are many women reading these words at this exact moment feeling the exact same way that you do right now. You are not alone here; this is a place of realization and reflection. It's time for you to start taking back your life, and it's time for you to take back the love you've wasted on all of those people who were never worthy. You got here because you desire something real, and you're here now because you realize that the person you thought to be the truth was lying all along, and that's the first step to moving on. Understanding that the person you want may not be the one you need and that person may never be capable of providing the type of love you deserve.

———

I hope you find yourself, and after you
rediscover who you are, I hope you
then find a love that enriches your
entire life. . . .

_____

she is culture
a representation
of all emotional
spiritual
and intellectual
achievements
collectively

she was art
before the paintings
she was genius
before the word

---

she saw magic
in her reflection
she healed herself
with a glance

———————————

you may take her for granted
you will lose her eventually
and you will remember her
whenever things go wrong

because it could have been beautiful
she wanted to be good to you
she was always good to you
but you lost her

———————————

girls like you
dance on their demons
girls like you
interrupt the devil's plans

_____

when it's too hot
she's the breeze
when you need air
she's what you'll breathe
be good to her

———————————

Thank you for showing me what true betrayal looks like. Instead of being the love of my life, you decided to be a lesson, and that's okay.

———————————

Acting like you don't need me. Just keep that same energy when I'm gone.

———————————

Never choose a fling over a lifetime.
Never neglect the ocean for a lake.

_____

I used to think I had issues controlling my anger until I realized that my biggest problem is that I've entertained people who have no concern over how their actions affect me. The people who push your buttons until they get the reaction they've been searching for are also the people who label you without holding themselves accountable for not being supportive of your desire to be at peace. The people who do the most to rob you of your peace are the ones who make you out to be a problem.

It's such an odd thing to be confronted with the fact that you can give seasons of love and devotion and peace to a person while they do everything in their power to disrupt that, and when their attempts work and they are successful at hurting you to the point of anger, they play the victim. But I'm learning that the only thing to do is to let go.

———————————

Change is scary but you deserve something different. Something better.

———————————

Peace is so fucking attractive.
_____

if they don't see it
fuck 'em
your magic
will only be visible
to those prepared
to appreciate it

———————————

her courage and wisdom, a mountain
unyielding, steadfast and profound
sculpted by heartache and time
weathering all storms

_____

her brilliance, a flame
fiercely radiating warmth
in the depths of winter
casting a light
that destroys darkness

_____

a woman's love is a lighthouse
piercing through dense fog
pathing a way
to those lost at sea

_____

she blooms through adversity
a rare force of nature
beyond and greater
than anything
anyone could ever imagine
she is you

———————————————

her heart
was the shape of the moon
her love was a gentle light
in darkness

——————————————

she moved with a silent eloquence
her dance, the sound of the harp singing
a song of love, self-love
and devotion
to what kept her mind at peace

———————————

she, in life's ballet
a ballerina made of bamboo
bending without breaking
dancing through the wind
rooted in self-love

_____

brilliant like the northern lights
she is mesmerizing
filling a midnight sky
with vibrant hues
of strength and love

―――――――――――――

seeds can't flourish
in a garden
nurtured by lies

_____

Being in an unhealthy relationship distorts the image of self, which causes us to question our own worth.

Unhealthy relationships burn like a fire with no control, consuming all hope and leaving behind sadness made of ash.

Once you're betrayed by the one you love, the trust you have for them becomes a bridge made of brittle sticks. Unsafe, unstable. Threatening to collapse under the weight of every suspicious act.

---

it wasn't love; it was a lesson

_____

a woman's skin is magic in every shade

_____

after all this time
searching for true love
she realized
that she was just waiting
for herself

_____

There's a difference between a man who sees you as a person and a man who sees you as pussy. . . .

It's all in the way he treats you. For sex, a man will do anything and say anything to you in the beginning. Make you feel good or even spark the potential of something long-term just to get what he wants. You see, chances are you're single or available because you've been through some tough things in a previous relationship. He doesn't need to ask you this to know it to be true. It's an assumption that is often spot-on, and so he knows how to approach it in an effort to get closer to what he wants, and once he gets it, if he doesn't see you as a person, he'll never truly respect you as one, and so begins the cycle of confusion. He's nice, kind, and more open when he wants you to be open to giving him what he wants, and when he's ready for something else, he'll push you away to provide space to do as he pleases without your watchful eye or to avoid any questioning.

Years of a series of long-term relationships have taught me that you can't rely on someone else to define your self-worth, and no amount of love will open the eyes of someone who is comfortable with seeing you as less than you are. You have to be present, focused, and mindful, eyes and heart open to the truth that sits in front of you. It's normal to be blinded by the energy and actions that reside mostly at the beginning of a relationship. It's easy to remain blinded by the potential your partner has or by what and who you think they can be. Choosing reality over the fantasy you've created in your heart is essential. Choosing the truth means preserving the best version of your future. Holding on to someone who best fits in your past destroys every chance you have at finding genuine love. It's time to let them go so that you can set yourself free.

The longer you remain in a relationship with the wrong person, the more you forget what your heart deserves. The more you settle, the further you are from a love that makes sense.

_____

Stop waiting for inspiration. Look inward and feel inspired.

———————————

she is a fire
stuck between
the desire to keep you warm
and the need to burn you
out of her heart

_____

having faith in someone
doesn't mean anything
if that someone
has no faith in themselves

_____

i'm not perfect
but i'm just trying
to give you more reasons
to love me than reasons to leave

——————————

we stood there
surrounded by nature
and there was this moment
where i watched her
marvel at the cherry blossoms
and i thought to myself
she's come home
to say hello

———————————

she sang
love songs
with her presence

to be near her
was to live in the notes
of a wild
and beautiful melody

_____

i always come to her
because wildflowers
belong among the woods
meadows, wetlands,
and mountains

———————————

there's something about her aura
that tells me that a moment beside her
feels like forever

_____

the girl with the highest walls
put too many of the wrong hearts
ahead of her own

———————————————

i want to love her
first thing in the morning
with wild hair
and tired eyes
before her lips are glossy
and her skin is dewy

i want to love her
first thing in the morning
before she attempts
to be more beautiful
than she already is

_____

when she smiled
the stars
burned bright
with envy

————————————

they sowed seeds
of betrayal
and deceit
a harvest of sadness
took root in your soul

———————————

you are a beacon
a magnificent light
far too radiant
for most men
to comprehend

———————————————

in quiet suffering
that fractured smile
still echoed love
and while some see damage
i see the love of my life

_____

silence is a poet
the way it gently whispers
a truth that your heart
is not ready to hear

———————————

she is becoming
more aware
of what honestly
deserves her energy
and this is her rediscovering
what it means to be powerful

_____

being selective
is a practice
in self-care

_____

she is a quiet visionary
silently building a future
that has no room
for the people
who made her
question herself

_____

leaving is painful
but so is fighting
to hold
the wrong relationship
together

_____

your path feels difficult
because you're trying
to walk beside people
who don't deserve
space in your journey

_____

you had to be broken
to finally realize
how capable you are
at rebuilding yourself

_____

i had to leave you
to reconnect with myself

_____

you ended the cycle
don't let the fear of loneliness
drive you back to a relationship
that makes you feel alone

_____

she was distant
because she had no time
to waste on people
who made no time for her

_____

they question your loyalty
but here you are
keeping secrets for people
who have decided to betray you

_____

no matter what ends
i am always okay
no matter the ending
i will always start over

_____

perfection wasn't expected
i just wanted you to be good

—————————————————

stop relying on people
to love you
you find true love
when you realize
that you are capable
of completing yourself

———————————

sometimes your ex
is not something to get over
sometimes your ex
is a lesson to think through
you learn then leave

———————————————

even the kindest people
get tired of the bullshit

_____

when you decide to love once more
i hope your heart falls into soft hands
willing to fight for your love

————————————————

in the orchestra of existence
she is a symphony
her melody a blend
of genius and strength

———————————

she didn't want to fit
into the algorithm
the only engagement
she was after
is the kind that happens
unplugged
undistracted
offline

———————————

she cried; the type of rivers
that carved canyons
the pain in her heart
was transformative
the sadness in her soul
eventually
made all things beautiful

_____

sometimes you have to
walk through the rain
to find a thunderous love

_____

in the symphony of her soul
lies a song of resilience

_____

she burned bridges
to illuminate her journey
toward something better

_____

she built her castle
from the ruins
of her own heart
because she realized
that she'd be
the safest home
for herself

———————————

each heartbreak is a wave
she's learning how to swim

_____

she's searching for a love
that understands her silence

_____

self-love
is a fortress
that protects
the heart

_____

she is like the moon
going through phases
of emptiness and sorrow
until she is whole again

———————————

your body
a love letter
sometimes
given to the
wrong person

_____

she wasn't really depressed
she was just self-aware

_____

i think it's brave
the way you love freely
even when you feel unwanted
and i hope you realize
that you deserve someone
who has enough courage
to love you back

———————————

she has a passionate longing
for a lasting love
and while she built walls
in front of her heart
she knew deep down
that anyone worth loving
would see this wall
as a reason to fight
for her love and devotion

———————————————

she is more than a moment
she's a forever kind of gal

_____

how could she ever fear the night
when she's befriended the moon

_____

her love is young and wild
her soul is vintage
her heart feels safe
she's the woman
you paint forevers with

_____

the wild thing is
you made her feel
as if she were nothing
you treated her
like she was never enough
and still, she's your biggest loss

———————————

it's beautiful
the way she takes
the chaos in her heart
and mixes it with poetry

_____

stop trying to show your heart
to people who can't comprehend
anything beyond your skin

———————————————

she was shy
and still
she was curious
about love
despite the warnings
of the heartbreak
that may follow
and i hope that curiosity
survives the saddest
moments of her life
because in the end
she deserves to be loved

———————————

they tried to replace you
don't let them wander
back into your life
after they failed

———————————————

she's the type of woman you miss
way before you've even met her
she lives in your dreams
because you can't fathom
her existence in this life
but she does

and if she thinks you're worthy
of her presence
never lose her
cherish her heart

———————————

you deserve to experience
the level of love you've given

———————————

she burned bridges
because she knew
that the fire
would purify her life

———————————

some see rain
as a reason
to run for cover
but to her
the storm is nurturing
and each raindrop
will inspire her to bloom

———————————

his words are never
more important
than his actions

pay attention

—————————————

getting over something
doesn't mean
you have to forget

_____

too often
you've seen forever
in eyes that never
intended to stay

you see their potential
even when they
treat you like nothing

you see love
because you are love
and you are just hoping
to receive what you give
and what you are

_____

you are a fire
learning to keep warm
without burning yourself

———————————————

recognize that you
are the love
you need
and then
you will stop waiting
for someone
who isn't built like you

_____

don't let him use
your beauty against you
don't let him
compliment
himself into places
that he'll never deserve
to visit

_____

i thought you'd complete me
but you took something
when you left

_____

the more she cried
the further she was
from the thing
that broke her

her tears
meant emptying herself
of everything that hurt

_____

those "i miss you" texts
turn phones into
emotional grenades
your ex is the enemy
put it down, don't respond

_____

i could hear the sound of sadness
between her lips, inside her voice
she spoke like a piece
of melancholy poetry
translucent and delicate
i fixated on every word

—————————————

but i hope you realize
that your tears
are quiet storms
washing away
what doesn't belong

_____

your heart is straining
because you're trying
to hold and lift
the relationship by yourself
and even though you
are strong enough to do it
you shouldn't be
doing this alone

———————————

i hope that when they remember
what is missing most in their lives
they'll think about you
while you've already moved on
to something better

_____

she isn't just the moon
but the entire galaxy
an infinite mystery
existing in a beautiful
dark sky

_____

her voice
a profound melody
that the stars
themselves dance to

her presence a song
that is best heard
in the depths of midnight

———————————

like the moon
hiding half of itself
she remained whole
even when she appeared
to be broken

———————————

she's the poet of her own life
each moment of the day
the song of her existence
writes a verse
a beautiful and enchanting anthology
of her existence

_____

each of her dreams
were stars
and every night
she slept
she painted a galaxy
on the canvas
of the universe

———————————

she transformed
each silence
into a symphony
weaving stories
of self-love
in the quiet
of heartbreak

_____

the wildness in her soul
rivals with a pack of wolves
_____

she was twilight
the way she maintained
the balance of her strength
and courage
between night and day

———————————

her heart is a nebula
her love gives birth
to the stars
her existence
interstellar
her presence
a new awakening
a space of profound
creation

_____

you thought she'd be hurt forever
you thought the door
would always be open
but what you never understood
was that she was an architect of time
and so she cultivated the space and time
to fall back in love with herself
so that her heart could fall away from you

————————————————

you see, it was more than sadness
the pain in her heart
caused her understanding to expand
and so, with every betrayal
she is wiser
with every heartbreak
she is more than she's ever been
and in the end
she realizes that she is better off
without the people
who inflicted that pain

———————————

but the thing you didn't realize
is that she's a lighthouse
and she was willing to guide you
through some of your darkest moments
but you lost her, and every time
you struggle against the shade of the night
you will discover that her love was a truth
you chose not to appreciate

———————————————

the only way to stimulate
the core of a woman's soul
is by earning her trust
and nurturing your promises
with your actions

———————————

a woman's peace is a prism
her joy is protection for self
and the ones who live in her heart
do only the things that make
her heart smile
do most of the things
that make her laugh
and she will protect you

—————————————

she, a gentle and fierce wind
shaping the world around her
her presence, one of creation
her energy, one of strength

———————————

she was a wildflower
deeply rooted in the earth
reaching toward the stars
telling stories to the moon

_____

Relationships are gardens that need to be nurtured with patience and tender devotion to grow and bloom.

————————————

In truth, depression has always felt like a cold dark night, but every night leads to a new dawn. The dark is transformed by light.

———————————

Sometimes, loneliness can feel like a mountain, but even so, the peak of that mountain allows you to see the world.

Take your time.

_____

in your search for truth
you will discover
many people
who will break
the silent promise of trust
but you'll also discover
what and who to avoid
moving forward

———————————

she stood alone
like a midnight moon
dressed in darkness
and yet she lit the world

_____

Sometimes the deepest scars are the ones you carry within your heart; sometimes, those scars never completely heal; you just learn to move forward stronger than you were. You figure out new ways to survive, to begin again despite those wounds.

———————————

she embraces the storm
because she deserves
the rainbow that follows

_____

when you choose your own path
you may find that the road
isn't large enough to include
the people and things
you thought you needed
and that's okay
go alone

_____

I think that's what made her appear so
beautifully—the way she didn't let the
darkness of her past overshadow the
light that resided within her heart.

———————————————

women like you are brave
they love fiercely
because of who they are inside
despite the chances
of having their heart broken
and even though i hate
to see you in pain
it's that ability to love
without conditions
that makes you beautiful

———————————————

I know what he did to you broke your heart, and I can understand why you'd lose sleep over someone you cared about even when they didn't care the same. But I also hope that you know that no amount of heartbreak will stand in the way of the genuine love you deserve. I hope something good finds you because you've been through so much in your search for real love. I hope someone looks upon you with the realization that you alone are more than enough, and, until then, I just want you to begin falling in love with yourself again. Right now, you deserve YOU more than anything. I really hope these words reach the right heart, the one who needs it the most . . . you.

———————————

one day her mind
and her heart
will reunite
and she will discover
the difference
between what she felt
and how things
had always been
the mind knew
what to do
but the heart
was too stubborn

---

i used to think
that the modern world
offered many opportunities
to connect
but as i look around
at all the faces
buried in a screen
i realized something
that we remain separated
by the very things
that used to help us
reach one another
distracted by the very thing
that was supposed to help us
free up more time
to focus on what really matters

———————————————

stop taking relationship advice
from people who have never really been in one
marriage advice can't be given
by an internet guru who has never been a spouse
stop looking for answers in a device
that is home to people
who have no real clarity of their own
pick up a book for content
stop reaching for your phone

_____

remember when self-care
meant logging off
now it's just content
now it's just performative
we used to sign out
in search of love for self
instead, we sign on
in search of likes
and engagement

———————————

everyone is rare
while doing the same shit

_____

be true to yourself
but only if it fits
the interest of an algorithm

———————————

self-care, self-love
keep scrolling, keep scrolling

mental health for more engagement

your mental health is content
what an unhealthy way to live

———————————————

of course, love is blind
the heart
has no eyes

_____

when i do it
it's wrong
when you do it
it's a mistake

———————————

sometimes healing
is what happens
when nothing else can

_____

she walked through the fire
like a poem touching flames

———————————————

if it wants to leave
let it go
if it wants to return
remember why it left

_____

set boundaries, Queen
and let go of anyone
who can't follow
the rules

———————————

she just wants someone
who can comprehend
every mood that lives
in her heart

———————————————

stop overplaying
your part
in the life of someone
who isn't matching
your effort

_____

i hate that it hurt you
my truth, my inability to lie
you wanted more
than i could give
you deserved more
than i could be
i let go
to set you free

———————————————

i was nothing
like the dream
you were dreaming
our reality plagued
by my refusal
to accept
the love in your heart
and i'm sorry
i didn't
love me enough
to see what you saw in me

_____

it was never you
your imperfections
were all beautiful
i just couldn't get over
the things i'd been through
before you entered my life

_____

Like the moon, your strength may be full or barely visible, but it never leaves your side.

———————————

In a world of delicate glass, she is iron and steel.

_____

She is a desert rose, blooming despite
the storm.

_____

She wasn't afraid of the chaos because
her heart was a supernova; her origin,
a star born from violent and powerful
explosions.

_____

Though she has grown familiar with the dark, she has chosen to be defined by the light she cultivates.

_____

she wasn't the damsel
she was the dragon

_____

every scar is a testament
to the battles you've won

_____

he tried to craft a cage
to keep her hidden
without understanding
that nothing human-made
could conquer a goddess

_____

she found every piece
of her broken heart
and used the fragments
to forge a crown

———————————

broken is not her legacy
broken was a lesson
broken is the feeling
that taught her
how to be resilient

———————————

she looked at the storm
and saw herself

_____

you are not an echo
you are the source

_____

your body is not a bargaining chip for validation and love
your body is not a bargaining chip for validation and love
your body is not a bargaining chip for validation and love

———————————————

She is not a mirror reflecting the
social expectations of an algorithm;
she is fire, a flame encased in a prism
refracting her own light. Choosing to
be seen for who she truly is.

———————————————

you pushed her into the deep end
expecting she'd drown
but as she fell toward the water
she fell into herself

_____

she had always been an untamed garden
with no desire for perfection
she bloomed wild and free

_____

you're single because
you were with someone
who draped sadness over your heart
you're single because
you know that loneliness
should not grow
within a relationship

———————————

in every kiss
he sews a path of emptiness
an aching of the heart
woven with a thread of silence
and betrayal hidden within
the fabric of everything
she believed to be real

———————————

in the cathedral of love
you were the only one
in the congregation
sitting alone in silence
waiting for the person
who promised to show up
but never did

———————————

the kisses were no longer
full of love's weight
the hugs grew weaker
and "i love you"
became a faint whisper
fading and distressed
over time

————————————

being in love
shouldn't make your heart
feel confined

———————————————

it's like we were stuck in rehearsal
our love, rarely on display
nearly never performed
a duet i sang alone

_____

your touch
reminds me
of how cold
it can get

_____

i thought i could love again
but fear caused me
to leave again

_____

you don't need to fit
into the algorithm to be seen
you don't need to fit
into the algorithm to be seen
you don't need to fit
into the algorithm to be seen
you don't need to fit
into the algorithm to be seen
you don't need to fit
into the algorithm to be seen
you don't need to fit
into the algorithm to be seen

———————————

i see you
i feel your eyes
dancing from left
to right

_____

i feel you
i feel you
i feel you
i feel you
i feel you
i feel you

———————————

your mind
at the edge
your heart
full of emptiness

_____

your eyes
filled with everything
you don't say
screaming in silence
searching for a way out

———————————

i see your hiding place
the secrets behind your face
your eyes swell
trying not to tell
the tales and the reasons
behind your sadness

---

i see you
i see you
i see you
i see you
i see you
i see you

———————————

fuck the algorithm
your heart is too big
to be reduced in size
to fit inside the data
that everyone else
is trying to live by

———————————

here's the thing
in the midnight
of your heartbreak
you will find pieces
of what is left
of your light
in the corners
of darkness
in places
where light
should not be able
to reach
but you will find
yourself there
between
the twilight
of night and day

———————————

you're just tired of the searching
the longing, the dreaming
the wanting, the needing
the overthinking, the fighting
the apologizing, the lying
the crying, the breaking
the taking, the waking
into another day
noon of sorrow
bleeding into night
the restlessness
the breathlessness
the near moment
of collapse
the struggle from within
the chill in the air
surrounding your body
you're just tired of the searching

there's a storm
dancing in the sky
the kettle is on
sitting gently
above a flame

there is chaos in the city
it's getting closer and closer
but there is a calm
sitting inside the chest
of the woman
reading these words

———————————

i dedicate this symphony to you
these words like a song
that will get stuck in your head
and dwell somewhere
deep within your soul

there is rain
falling out of love
with the sky
you see its drops
on glass, you hear its voice
whispering out to you
come home; you are also a storm
and today, you are a calm one

---

you are love in search of love
and somehow, you forgot
to give you to yourself

———————————

Of course, it's impossible to know what will come next, but if you focus on yourself and what you need, you will spend most of your time creating on your own everything you've waited for others to create with you.

———————————

Better to be single, refusing to compromise yourself for the approval of someone who doesn't deserve you.

_____

If they want to leave, let them. No sense in trying to keep an unkept version of love.

———————————

Don't let someone unworthy of your heart make you forget the value your heart brings to a relationship.

———————————

It's not a loss; it's relief.

_____

You have to be whole when alone so that you can identify and welcome whole love for someone else.

_____

Don't let your ex harden the softest
parts of your heart.

———————————

are you predicting the future
or is the future using
your predictions as inspiration

are you grateful for life
or is life grateful to have you

_____

don't let the algorithm define you
don't let the algorithm tell you
what to care about
or what's important
or what to be angry about
or who to be angry with
don't let the algorithm
shift your rhythm
don't let it dictate the direction
you're heading in
don't let it win
live above it, not inside it
live above it, not inside it
live above it, not inside it
love and peace are everywhere
you must log off to find it
log off to find it
log off to find you
log off, define you

When a relationship ends, it may
feel like a destructive moment for
the heart, but in time, you realize
that when the heart is broken,
it transforms into something
greater. The betrayal, the lies. The
disappointment will hurt at first, but
eventually the pain
becomes the reason why you
evolve and grow.

_____

I think you forget how strong you've always had to be. I think it hurts so much that you literally lose the understanding of your own capabilities, but you've been here before, and no matter how bad it gets, you have always figured out how to make it to the other side. Keep going—you got this.

_____

You are more than enough, even when the person you love refuses to match your dedication. You are worthy of love, even though it's been difficult searching for a love that meets your needs. Your heart remains beautiful even after it's been dragged through the ugliest of emotions. Give no one the power to dictate your worth and never blame yourself for someone's inability to appreciate all that you have to offer.

———————————

emerging from the embers and ashes
of past relationships
she is reborn, forged in fire
a phoenix without fear

_____

she, a lioness in the wild
thriving amid the unknown
fierce in protection
of her peace

_____

against the dark canvas of night
you glow with the courage of the moon
no fear of changing phases
brave enough to stand alone

———————————————

Healing will only begin when you decide that your peace of mind is more important than seeking closure from someone who was never sure about you and incapable of communicating their feelings for you. It can be hard to let go without closure, but you must remember that the person you want answers from was never good at being honest and up-front with you.

———————————

the end is not the end
the end is where you begin
goodbye means saying goodbye
to what has been keeping you
from yourself
goodbye is hello to better

_____

The opportunities are endless when you are single. The world opens up in preparation to welcome you back into a world where the main objective is to fully understand who you are and what you need either on your own or when you begin to search for someone new. Take advantage of this chance to truly see yourself for who you've always been and what you can become with some time to yourself.

———————————

Being single is not a punishment. It is a path leading you away from a relationship that feels like chaos when what you actually deserve is peace. There is no use for a relationship that causes you to feel all the things you've been trying to avoid. There is no point in running back into a relationship that requires you to feel a pain so deep that it distracts you from the joy you claim to want.

—————————————

Single life is a break from the drama
that is being with the wrong person.
When you are single, you have the
freedom to pour more of your energy
into cultivating the type of love you
believe you deserve. Being single
provides you with the time your heart
needs to heal and to trust again. Turn
that newfound trust inward and use
that newfound courage to prevent
yourself from settling.

———————————

Single life is the moment between heartbreak and a love worthy of your time and energy. The best way to make room for genuine love is to leave behind anyone who refuses to match your effort.

———————————————

The reward of being single is that you are readily available to fully experience the love in your heart. It is in this moment where you are free to pour all that you are into everything that is you. Being single is a time when you discover that you are everything you need and that you are capable of being a soulmate to yourself.

———————————

it wasn't easy
but i had to
leave you
so that my days
could be kinder
and my nights
more peaceful

———————————

to find a love
that remains the same
or better yet, expands
into more, is a dream
that seems so distant

_____

It's always interesting how the people you do the most for are the same ones who are first in line to make you feel less than you are. I have discovered this to be true several times over and in what I've felt are my most important relationships. I think it's sick, but I've also reached a point in my life where what used to hurt me is now received as a lesson plan on how to deal with certain people. It's a very important lesson in maintaining my peace of mind and the velocity with which I aim to love others going forward. I don't think it should change the way you love the people you meet in the future, but it does beg the question of why the people who should fear the loss of someone like you find it so easy to disregard and disrespect you.

———————————

this is not a drought
this is not your dry season
you just forgot that you are water
and that you are capable
of watering yourself

———————————

she wasn't really depressed
she was just self-aware

_____

please don't like the photos
more than you listen to the songs
please don't like the photos
more than you focus on the art
they are more than just their social
cherish the fact they let you in
but if you like the photo
more than you consume the art
the artist will never win

———————————————

you are gold
don't settle for shit

———————————

Stay away from people who go out of their way to hurt and upset you, then pretend to be the victim when you get tired of their shit.

_____

It's wild how you can change a person's entire life and they'll take that life and give it to everyone else but you.

_____

A lot of the photos you see on social media are just the highlights of a sad life.

_____

as long as they keep you confused
they keep you from leaving
as long as they keep you confused
you linger longer than you should
searching for an answer
in a place full of lies
you will never find clarity
in a relationship with someone
who'd rather see you blind

———————————

that's a pretty little thing
called a heart
tough but soft
alive and fighting
while it breaks
it makes you beautiful
despite the sorrow
it keeps you alive
despite the death of love
use it to get through
the thing that wants
to destroy it

---

he knows you'll want closure
he left you wondering
silently asking questions
that he'll never answer
because he knows
that you'll stay stuck
in a place where he left you
waiting for him to return
after he's done
exploring a relationship
with someone else

---

i miss the days
when an ordinary life
wasn't pressured to become content
or when conversations
were about things that mattered
rather than things that trend
i miss the days when leisure
was a way
to distance self from work
but now a vacation
is just a way to leverage a possible sponsor
it's wild the way we embraced technology
only to transform it into an impossible monster
and in all of human history, finding a mate
was never an issue
but now you're lost
in the web, and it's a shame
because i miss you
living by the algorithm
deciding to hide the real you
performative for likes
that's real engagement
for a fake you
pretending you're not an addict
as if this drug doesn't faze you

_____

in a symphony of sorrow
she played the violin
of resilience and courage

———————————

her soul learned how to dance
in a rhythm absent of fear
beneath thunderstorms of sorrow

——————— ———

like an ancient tree
she never yields
to the wind of heartbreak

———————————

it's interesting, really
the way a woman's tears
nurture the seeds of her soul
helping her grow
into a stronger woman

———————————

in the midst
of a hurricane
her heart
becomes a lighthouse

_____

rainstorms were always
just a drink to her
feeding her soul
she bloomed into a wildflower

———————————

standing beneath
a thunderstorm
a woman realizes
that she is the root
not a leaf

_____

in the garden of self
a woman determines
when and where to bloom

_____

in the quiet hours
beneath a full moon
an act of self-care
becomes a sweet symphony
she plays for herself

———————————————

she is better than beautiful
there's just something rare about her
too profound for words to express

———————————

sadness stumbled into my heart
like a wayward drunk
with regret on its breath
and lies on its tongue

———————————

depression had always felt
like an uninvited guest
or a shadow that refused to leave
in a corner where the sun
refused to shine

—————————————

solitude feels bitter
when you've been abandoned
but time alone gifts you
the courage to live a life
that thrives in the absence
of those who do not deserve
your presence and light

———————————

a sad heart
is a dusty
and worn-down attic
filled with ideas
that never reached
full potential
and love
that turned out
to be a lie
cluttered by
nightmarish dreams
and unfulfilled desire

_____

stop looking for answers
on tongues that lie
stop looking for safety
in harmful arms
stop searching for love
in a heart filled with hate
stop wanting the ones
who don't deserve you
stop thinking about people
who make you feel forgotten
stop making space
for those who don't make time
you have to stop doing for them
and start doing for yourself
you have to stop to start
you have to stop to start

———————————————

it's funny the way
the people who critique
your character
are the same ones
who are always
trying to provoke you
to become someone
you're not

it's wild the way
they label you angry
when they're the reason
for you feeling upset

and it's strange how
they prefer you
to react to their bullshit
with a calm and grace
that they never deserve

———————————

Why am I always the one apologizing to maintain the peace that you do not help support? Why am I always the one providing second chances to people who do not appreciate the first? Why must my heart suffer in the hands of someone who doesn't deserve it, and why am I so quick to forgive someone who punishes me for simply reacting to their bullshit?

You always come back around when you fail to replace me. So loud in the arguments, confident that you'll find better, but in time, you return with empty promises and lies disguised as apologies. My love weakens every time you return, begging for a place that you have proven unworthy of, the way you overexaggerate the good that you do or your importance in my life, but each time you leave, I realize more and more that there is a profound sense of peace whenever you're not around. I cease to question my self-worth, and there is no need to wonder whether or not what you say is true or just another lie. I love who I am without you, and one day, I won't be standing in the place you left me. One day my heart will have changed its locks, and you will truly understand what it is to lose the best thing you didn't deserve to receive in the first place.

———————

A Wildflower, FREE

written by r.h. Sin

INT. APARTMENT - NIGHT

The room is slightly lit by a lone lamp. The cityscape, along with tall, slender buildings, sends flashes of light through floor-to-ceiling windows.

EMMA (early 30s, restless but resilient) stands, wearily staring out the window of a shared apartment, cradling a photo of her and someone she believed she'd spend the rest of her life with. Her ex, initially charismatic and yet gentle in his presence, hiding behind gestures that at one time appeared genuine.

EMMA: (softly, speaking inward)

He managed to be both dusk and dawn. . . . A familiar scent in streets crowded with people. A soft and enchanting song on the most terrible of days . . . but what good is the melody when the lyrics eventually break you?

Struggling to pull her head out of the dark midnight clouds.

EMMA quietly, wearing a distressed look on her face, thinking to herself, "No, I can't believe I'm doing this to myself again."

Gently placing the photo face down on the side table. Rubbing her eyes in an effort to fight back the urge to cry.

EMMA: (speaking passionately)

He was a sweet yet poisonous nectar. And there were times when he'd light me up to the stars just to watch me fall. There were times when he'd make me feel love, and then without warning, render me worthless without any sign of remorse. It almost felt as if he believed that I deserved the pain, and I'd spent so much time questioning myself, believing it to be true, that whenever I looked into the mirror, my reflection agreed.

She takes a moment to notice her reflection in the window, her eyes meeting her face in search of some sign of strength.

EMMA: (whispering with confidence)

But I . . . I am not worthless. I am not the pain that they've forced me to feel. I am not someone who deserves to feel broken at the expense of someone's inability to be brave enough to fall in love.

(She takes a deep breath.)

Some of the sweetest lies ever told . . . he'd sold them all as truth. Laced with charm, a smile that turned out to be a mask, every word a drug, and I was surely addicted.

Her grip tightens on the windowsill, heart racing, nearly audible. Fingers aching.

EMMA: (determined and triumphant)

No. Fuck it. This . . . this ends now, for good. I can't change him, and I should not even have to try. If the love he spoke into me was real, that alone would have been enough for him to do better. I can't save him; I can't save us. . . . But I can save myself. In me lives the strength to put an end to this cycle.

She steps back from the window, taking a moment to steady herself, her resolve hardening.

EMMA: (fiercely with conviction and truth)

It will hurt. The nights will be long, filled with his phantom whispers. . . . And the days? Oh, they will be a maze, our shared memories waiting at every corner. But I will fight—for my worth, for my peace, for the love I deserve.

Fuck . . . this is going to hurt. The nights will often seem unending, filled with longing and phantom whispers that will prey upon the loneliness in the heart. And the days? The days will force me to navigate the maze of our shared memories, but I will fight with everything that I have to prove that I am worthy of peace and love. All the things that you were incapable of providing.

She grabs her coat from the back of a chair and heads to the entryway to open the door.

EMMA: (softly spoken as calm washes over her face)

I am stepping into the unknown, but at least it won't be the hell that I've known. There is a future beyond this moment, and I am ready to welcome it.

She reaches for the brass doorknob and exits the apartment, leaving behind the ghost of everything she believed her life could be. The door slowly closes behind her as if waving goodbye, echoing her final decision. The room stands still, quiet, emptier than it has ever been, waiting for a new chapter to begin.

FADE TO BLACK